THE FIRST GAME

Written by

ANDRIS BERKIS

Illustrated by Mauricio Loubet

US Version

Published by The Lion of Scandinavia Publishing

First published in 2024

Written by Andris Berkis
Illustrated by Mauricio Loubet
Book design by Bryony van der Merwe

ISBN: 978-91-989474-0-3 (hardcover)
ISBN: 978-91-989474-1-0 (paperback)
ISBN: 978-91-989474-2-7 (e-book)

www.thegreatforestleague.com

This book is dedicated to
my children
RALPH, ALEXANDER
and ODRIJA,
who inspired me to write
this story.

Many types of animals lived in the Great Forest. They sometimes bickered about territory and food, but they all agreed on their love of soccer. It was the best sport and an activity that united the forest.

"Let's have a tournament!" suggested Rosie of the Rabbits one sunny spring day. "A SOCCER TOURNAMENT!"

"That's a brilliant idea," agreed Brody of the Bears. "We can call it the Great Forest League!"

"We'll need time to prepare," added Walter of the Wolves. "Shall we set the games for summer?"

"Perfect," shrieked Henrietta of the Hedgehogs. "I CAN'T WAIT!"

SIX TEAMS decided to participate
in the first Great Forest League:
the Bears, Rabbits, Wolves, Foxes, Boars,
and Hedgehogs.

Excitedly, the teams began training.
By summer, they were ready for the
GREAT FOREST LEAGUE,

THE FIRST GAME was between the Bears and Rabbits. The forest bubbled with excitement. The game was to be played in a meadow in the forest. Many animals climbed the trees surrounding the meadow to see the game clearly.

Each team had a star player. For the Bears, this was BRODY, a stern-looking Bear who was their goalkeeper.

In the Rabbit team, ROSIE was the best striker. She moved so quickly, dribbling faster than the eye could see past opponents.

"We're going to win this game!" Rosie said to her team.

Her teammates cheered as they stepped onto the field.

On the other side stood the Bears.
"THIS GAME IS OURS," said Brody confidently.

The stands were filled with animals and birds,
all clamoring loudly for the game to start!

The Badgers were appointed as REFEREES...

and the Woodpeckers were
KEEPING SCORE.

GO!
GO!
The game started
with the Rabbits
playing out the
FIRST BALL.

the Rabbits launched into their attack, laid out carefully by Rosie. They moved swiftly around the Bear players.

Rosie received the ball in a fast run and then dribbled past the Bear defenders. Though they were much bigger than her, she wasn't intimidated.

"I may not be big, but I'M FAST," she thought as she neared the goal, where Brody awaited.

Rosie made a STRONG SHOT, but Brody was ready.

He leaped to the left, swiped the ball, and deflected the ball over the crossbar.

"HAH!" said Brody, feeling proud. The Rabbits would have to work harder if they wanted to score.

Rosie sighed and raced after the ball with the rest of the players. "No!" she cried as one of the Bears got hold of the ball and began to BUILD THEIR PLAY.

The Bears easily reached a position for a good shot at the goal, but the Rabbits' athletic goalkeeper made a SPECTACULAR SAVE.

"YES! WELL DONE!" Rosie and her team cheered.

After both teams had exchanged well-played attacks that resulted in no goals, the score was still 0:0, and the spectators were **GETTING LOUDER.**

Then the breaking moment came—
one of the Bear players near their own
goal tackled a player from the Rabbit
team. The tackle was too strong, and
the spectators held their breath. The
whistle blew as the referee awarded the
Rabbits a PENALTY KICK.

Rosie stepped up to take the penalty.
With a running start and weaving
movements, she confused Brody. He
didn't know which way she would go.
After the strike, the ball hit the upper
corner of the goal—the Rabbit team
had scored the first goal in the Great
Forest League.

"I DID IT! I DID IT!" she shouted, hugging
her teammates.

Although both teams had chances to score before the break, the first half ended with a score of 1:0 IN FAVOR OF THE RABBITS.

The result was UNEXPECTED for the Bears and the audience. The Bears had come to the game confident that with their strength, they would easily overpower the quick, agile, but smaller Rabbits.

 the Bears' coach, the oldest Bear in the Great Forest, paced along the Bear's bench.

"What are we going to do?" he wondered.

Brody was worried, like the rest of his teammates.

Suddenly, the coach said, "I have an idea. Gather around."

As he explained his idea, Brody smiled. The Rabbits would be surprised by this play!

As the game resumed, it quickly became clear that the Bears had changed their way of playing. They played very strangely—several Bear players surrounded the one with the ball.

Although it wasn't a beautiful soccer play, their new plan was effective—the Rabbit team players couldn't get close enough to get the ball. And then the Bears scored!

 argued Rosie, but it was. She was just upset the Bears were doing so well.

Soon, the Bears scored their second goal.

By using confusion in Rabbits teams, the Bears quickly scored a third time—now the score was 3:1 in favor of the Bears.

The Rabbit team captain, their outstanding goalkeeper, quickly gathered his players for a quick meeting during a short break.

"LISTEN UP. I have a plan," he said and began his explanation.

Rosie grinned. They would turn the game with this plan.

The new Rabbit GAME PLAN was simple—to not allow the Bear players to pass the ball to each other.

Using speed and agility, the Rabbits intercepted the ball before it reached the Bear midfielders and strikers. This allowed for COUNTERATTACKS.

"BEAT THAT!" Rosie shouted at Brody.

"There's time left. We will win!" roared Brody.

The spectators witnessed a truly thrilling first game of the Great Forest League—both Bears and Rabbits had adapted their game, resulting in an exciting forest soccer match. The forwards of both teams showed their speed and technique, the midfielders created plays, and the defenders successfully disrupted the opponent's attacks.

Both goalkeepers also had their paws full. Brody was saving every attempt the Rabbits made at trying to score, and the Rabbit captain MOVED SO FAST, trying to stop the Bears from scoring.

It seemed that the first game of the Great Forest League would end in a draw. However, shortly before the end of the game, the Rabbits managed to cross into the Bears' PENALTY AREA.

Although it was rare for the Rabbits to win high balls against the big Bears, this time, SOMETHING UNEXPECTED HAPPENED— a Rabbit forward surprised everyone.

Rosie! There she was. Following the cross, she performed a backward kick over her head—the so-called 'BICYCLE KICK',

The athletic jump and strike were SPECTACULAR and precise. The Rabbit team and their supporters again erupt in exciting celebrations.

The score was now 4:3 in favor of the Rabbit team.

In the game's final moments, the Bears managed one more good attack—after several successful passes, a Bear striker found himself in an excellent position to shoot from the left side. However, the Rabbit goalkeeper once again demonstrated his skills, beautifully saving the shot in the upper corner of the goal.

The game ended with an unexpected victory for the Rabbit team—4-3.

"WE WON, WE WON!" cheered Rosie together with her team.

The spectators stayed in the forest meadow for long afterward, loudly discussing the game. The first Great Forest League game had been a great success—both teams played exciting forest animal soccer.

THE SOCCER FEVER in the Great Forest had begun.

Read about the next game in

WOLVES VS FOXES

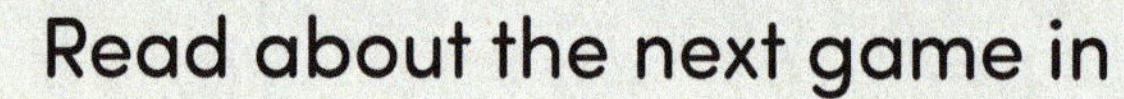

Follow the author online for information
about upcoming books and more.

www.thegreatforestleague.com